ACHIEVE

The expected standard

Reading

SATs Revision

**Laura Collinson
& Shareen Mayers**

RISING STARS

The Publishers would like to thank the following for permission to reproduce copyright material:

Photo credits
Photos from iStock: p9 bus © RTimages; p13 clock © mladn61; p15 snow shovel © wwing; p19 candle © RTimages; p21 chocolate © sumnersgraphicsinc; p23 fossil © Fyletto; p24 car © schlol; p25 watch © Gary Alvis; p27 goat © Antagain; pp29, 40 © dragon Sylphe_7; p31 gingerbread house © RuthBlack; p33 acorn © tomashkop; p35 horse © Lorado; p39 stack of books © skodonnell; p41 heart © Grotmarsel; p43 witch on broomstick © shelma1; p44 gift © dejan750; p45 snake © futureimage; p49 black cat © GlobalP; p51 plums © Anna Kucherova; p53 puppies © Alona Rjabceva; p54 dinosaur © Syldavia; p55 butterfly © fototdietrich; p57 toothpaste © mphillips007

Text extracts
p8 Chocolate teapot, by Paul Harris © *Mail Online*; p10 Reprinted with permission of Bishopsteignton Outdoor Art Group; p11, 23 Text reproduced from *The Usborne Science Encyclopaedia* by permission of Usborne Publishing, 83–85 Saffron Hill, London EC1N 8RT, UK www.usborne.com. Text copyright © 2009 by Kirsteen Robson; p11, 20, 36 Extract from *Monster Slayer* Copyright © 1999 Brian Patten, published by permission of Barrington Stoke Ltd; p12 *What Mr Darwin Saw* by Mick Manning and Brita Granstrom, published by Frances Lincoln Ltd, copyright © 2010. Reproduced by permission of Frances Lincoln Ltd, an imprint of The Quarto Group; p13 'Keeping your child quiet with a computer could WRECK their eyesight' by Helen Carroll © *Mail Online*; p14 From Tiggywinkles Wildlife Hospital Issue 72. Reprinted with permission; p15 *Polar Survival Handbook*, copyright © Miles Kelly Publishing Ltd 2012; Climate Change and Global Warming © Dr Kerry Kriger, www.savethefrogs.com/climate; p19 'A Spell to Cure Sorrow and Create Joy' reprinted with permission of Clare Bevan; *The Magician's Nephew* by C.S. Lewis copyright © C.S. Lewis Pte. Ltd. 1950. Extract reprinted by permission; p21 Roald Dahl article, reprinted with permission of *First News*; p23 *Five Tales from Shakespeare*, © Meg Harris Williams; p24 Text reproduced from *The Story of Cars* by permission of Usborne Publishing, 83–85 Saffron Hill, London EC1N 8RT, UK. www.usborne.com. Text copyright © 2008 by Katie Daynes; p25 *Darke Academy*, by Gabriella Poole. First published in the UK by Hodder Children's Books, an imprint of Hachette Children's Books, Carmelite House, 50 Victoria Embankment, London imprint, EC4Y 0DZ. Reproduced by permission; p26 Roller coasters extract, reprinted with permission of *First News*; p27 Excerpt from *The Shaman's Apprentice: A Tale of the Amazon Rain Forest* by Lynne Cherry and Mark J. Plotkin. Text copyright © 1998 by Lynne Cherry and Mark J. Plotkin. Reprinted with permission of Houghton Mifflin Harcourt Publishing. All rights reserved; *Shipwrecked! The Orchard Book of Heroes & Villains*, by Tony Bradman and Tony Ross. First published in the UK by Hodder Children's Books, an imprint of Hachette Children's Books, Carmelite House, 50 Victoria Embankment, London imprint, EC4Y 0DZ. Reproduced by permission; p28, 42 *Treasure Island*, by Robert Louis Stevenson; p29 *How to Train Your Dragon*, by Cressida Cowell. First published in the UK by Hodder Children's Books, an imprint of Hachette Children's Books, Carmelite House, 50 Victoria Embankment, London imprint, EC4Y 0DZ. Reproduced by permission; 'The Caractacus Chariot Company' reprinted with permission of Dr Mike Johnson; p30 'The Secret Diary of a Dragon' by Sheila Simmons; p31 'The Advertisement' from *This Poem Doesn't Rhyme*, by C. J. D. Doyle; 'Reasons to live near a volcano' www.geography-site.co.uk; p32 *The Selfish Giant and Other Stories*, by Oscar Wilde; p33 'Squirrels' reproduced with permission of Celia Warren; p34 'Did you Know' www.didyouknow.it; p35 'Study maths and science for space jobs, urges astronaut' by Anna Davis. Reprinted with permission; *Farm Boy*, by Michael Morpurgo © Pavilion Books Company Ltd; p37 'Autumn Breeze' by Patricia Garcia; p39 'Have a Great Day' EreadingWorksheets.com. Reproduced with permission of Donald E. Morton; p40 Hiccup interview, reprinted with permission of *First News*; p41 'Flooding' EreadingWorksheets.com. Reproduced with permission of Donald E. Morton; p45 *Macbeth*, by William Shakespeare; p47, 49 *The Lion, the Witch and the Wardrobe* by C.S. Lewis copyright © C.S. Lewis Pte. Ltd. 1950. Extract reprinted by permission; p48 'Rainbows' from *Paint a Poem*, by Moira Andrew; p50 'The Night is a Big Black Cat' by G. Orr Clark; 'Sea Shoal See Shows on the Sea Bed' reproduced with permission of Paul Cookson; p52, 53 *The Iron Man*, by Ted Hughes. Published by Faber and Faber, and Harper Collins US; p52 *A Sudden Puff of Glittering Smoke* by Anne Fine. Reprinted with permission of Anne Fine agency, David Higham Associates; p53 *Matilda* by Roald Dahl. Reprinted with permission of Roald Dahl, David Higham Associates; p54 *The Bright Pavilions*, by Hugh Walpole; p55 'Did this dinosaur nest have a 'babysitter'?' by Ellie Zolfagharifard © *Mail Online*; p56 'Fireworks' EreadingWorksheets.com. Reproduced with permission of Donald E. Morton; p58 From *Revenge of the Lunch Ladies: The Hilarious Book of School Poetry* by Kenn Nesbitt, Mike Gordon, and Carl Gordon, copyright © 2007. Reprinted by permission of Running Press, an imprint of Hachette Book Group, Inc; 'Toothpaste' by Michael Rosen (© Michael Rosen, 1979) is printed by permission of United Agents (www.unitedagents.co.uk) on behalf of Michael Rosen.

Every effort has been made to trace all copyright holders, but if any have been inadvertently overlooked, the Publishers will be pleased to make the necessary arrangements at the first opportunity.

Although every effort has been made to ensure that website addresses are correct at time of going to press, Rising Stars cannot be held responsible for the content of any website mentioned in this book. It is sometimes possible to find a relocated web page by typing in the address of the home page for a website in the URL window of your browser.

Hachette UK's policy is to use papers that are natural, renewable and recyclable products and made from wood grown in sustainable forests. The logging and manufacturing processes are expected to conform to the environmental regulations of the country of origin.

Orders: please contact Bookpoint Ltd, 130 Park Drive, Milton Park, Abingdon, Oxon OX14 4SE. Telephone: (44) 01235 400555. Email: primary@bookpoint.co.uk

Lines are open from 9 a.m. to 5 p.m., Monday to Saturday, with a 24-hour message answering service. Visit our website at www.risingstars-uk.com for details of the full range of Rising Stars publications.

Online support and queries email: onlinesupport@risingstars-uk.com

ISBN: 978 1 51044 248 1

© Hodder & Stoughton Limited 2018

First published in 2015

This edition published in 2018 by Hodder & Stoughton Limited (for its Rising Stars imprint, part of the Hodder Education Group),

An Hachette UK Company

Carmelite House

50 Victoria Embankment

London EC4Y 0DZ

www.risingstars-uk.com

Impression number   10 9 8 7 6

Year   2024   2023   2022   2021   2020

Authors: Laura Collinson and Shareen Mayers

Author (pages 18–19, 38–45): Ione Branton

Series Editor: Helen Lewis

Accessibility Reviewer: Vivien Kilburn

Cover design: Burville-Riley Partnership

Illustrations by John Storey

Typeset in India

Printed in Great Britain by Ashford Colour Press Ltd.

A catalogue record for this title is available from the British Library.

Contents

Welcome to Achieve Reading: The Expected Standard – Revision

In this book you will find all the activities and information you need to achieve the expected standard in the Key Stage 2 Reading test.

About the Key Stage 2 Reading National Test

The test will take place in the summer term in Year 6. It will be done in your school and will be marked by examiners – not by your teacher.

In the test you will be given a booklet containing a range of texts and another booklet for your answers. The texts will be from fiction, non-fiction and poetry. The first text will be the easiest and the last text will be the most challenging. The texts and questions will be very similar to the texts that you have been reading in school. You will have one hour to read the texts and complete the answer booklet.

The test is worth a total of 50 marks.

- Some questions ask you to find the answer in the text. These questions are usually worth 1 mark. These make up 44–66% of the marks.
- Some questions ask you to write a short answer. These questions are usually worth 2 marks. They make up 20–40% of the marks.
- Other questions ask you to write a longer answer. These are worth 3 marks. They make up 6–24% of the marks.

Test techniques

Before the test

- Try to revise little and often, rather than in long sessions.
- Choose a time of day when you are not tired or hungry.
- Choose somewhere quiet so you can focus.
- Revise with a friend. You can encourage and learn from each other.
- Read the 'Top tips' throughout this book to remind you of important points in answering test questions.
- Use the advice given in this book when you are reading your own reading book. Ask yourself some of the questions as you read along.
- KEEP READING all kinds of non-fiction, fiction and poetry texts.

During the test

- READ THE QUESTION AND READ IT AGAIN.
- If you find a question difficult to answer, move on; you can always come back to it later.
- Always answer a multiple-choice question. If you really can't work out an answer, read the text again and try to think of the most sensible response.
- Check to see how many marks a question is worth. Have you written enough to 'earn' those marks in your answer?
- Read the question again after you have answered it. Check you have done what the question asked you to do.
- If you have any time left at the end, go back to the questions you have missed.

Where to get help

- Pages 8–58 will help you develop the skills you need to achieve a scaled score of 100 in the test.
- Page 59 contains a glossary to help you understand key terms about writing, reading and grammar.
- Pages 63–64 provide the answers to the 'Try this' questions.
- Inside back cover contains a revision checklist to help you keep track of your progress.

How to use this book

1 *Introduction* – This section introduces each assessable element so you know what you need to achieve.

2 *What you need to know* – Important facts about the assessable elements are given in this section. Read them carefully. Words in purple are defined in the glossary at the back of the book.

3 *Let's practise* – This section includes short extracts from the types of text you can expect to find in the Key Stage 2 Reading National Test, as well as an example question. Follow the steps carefully and work through the example.

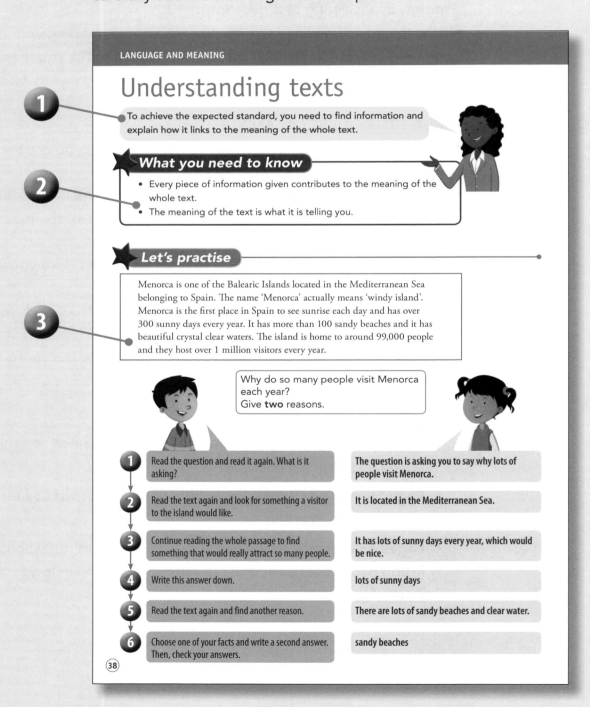

LANGUAGE AND MEANING

Understanding texts

1 To achieve the expected standard, you need to find information and explain how it links to the meaning of the whole text.

What you need to know

2
- Every piece of information given contributes to the meaning of the whole text.
- The meaning of the text is what it is telling you.

Let's practise

3 Menorca is one of the Balearic Islands located in the Mediterranean Sea belonging to Spain. The name 'Menorca' actually means 'windy island'. Menorca is the first place in Spain to see sunrise each day and has over 300 sunny days every year. It has more than 100 sandy beaches and it has beautiful crystal clear waters. The island is home to around 99,000 people and they host over 1 million visitors every year.

Why do so many people visit Menorca each year?
Give **two** reasons.

1 Read the question and read it again. What is it asking?

The question is asking you to say why lots of people visit Menorca.

2 Read the text again and look for something a visitor to the island would like.

It is located in the Mediterranean Sea.

3 Continue reading the whole passage to find something that would really attract so many people.

It has lots of sunny days every year, which would be nice.

4 Write this answer down.

lots of sunny days

5 Read the text again and find another reason.

There are lots of sandy beaches and clear water.

6 Choose one of your facts and write a second answer. Then, check your answers.

sandy beaches

38

4 Try this – Practise answering the questions for yourself.

5 Glossary – A glossary for some practice tests is provided to help with tricky words.

6 Top tips – These hints help you to do your best. Use them well.

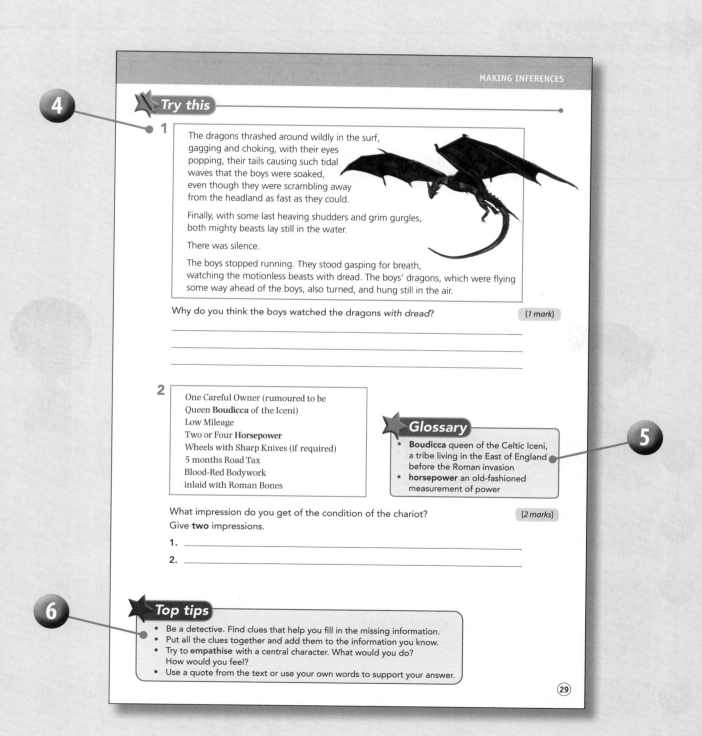

MAKING INFERENCES

Try this

4

1

The dragons thrashed around wildly in the surf, gagging and choking, with their eyes popping, their tails causing such tidal waves that the boys were soaked, even though they were scrambling away from the headland as fast as they could.

Finally, with some last heaving shudders and grim gurgles, both mighty beasts lay still in the water.

There was silence.

The boys stopped running. They stood gasping for breath, watching the motionless beasts with dread. The boys' dragons, which were flying some way ahead of the boys, also turned, and hung still in the air.

Why do you think the boys watched the dragons *with dread*? [1 mark]

_____

_____

_____

2

One Careful Owner (rumoured to be Queen **Boudicca** of the Iceni)
Low Mileage
Two or Four **Horsepower**
Wheels with Sharp Knives (if required)
5 months Road Tax
Blood-Red Bodywork
inlaid with Roman Bones

Glossary

5

- **Boudicca** queen of the Celtic Iceni, a tribe living in the East of England before the Roman invasion
- **horsepower** an old-fashioned measurement of power

What impression do you get of the condition of the chariot? [2 marks]
Give **two** impressions.

1. _____

2. _____

Top tips

6

- Be a detective. Find clues that help you fill in the missing information.
- Put all the clues together and add them to the information you know.
- Try to **empathise** with a central character. What would you do? How would you feel?
- Use a quote from the text or use your own words to support your answer.

(29)

Understanding words in context

To achieve the expected standard, you need to give the meaning of words in **context**.

 What you need to know

- Some words or groups of words can mean different things depending on the **context** in which they are written.

Let's practise

> Ever since humans embarked on the ceaseless quest for knowledge there have been questions that don't really need answers. Yesterday, some of the finest minds in science, engineering and craftsmanship combined to examine one of them anyway: precisely how useless is a chocolate teapot?

Yesterday, some of the finest minds…

What does the word *finest* mean in the second sentence?

Tick ✔ **one**.

luxury ☐   smallest ☐

clearest ☐   brightest ☐

1 Read the question and read it again. What is it asking?

The question is asking you to choose an alternative word from a given list.

2 Insert each word in turn in the sentence to replace *finest*. Read the sentence back to yourself each time.

luxury minds   smallest minds
clearest minds   brightest minds

3 Do not stop before the end of the list because you think you may have found the answer. Another word later in the list may be closer in meaning than the one you have chosen.

Yesterday, some of the brightest minds …

4 Check your answer.

The word that fits the best and is closest in meaning is *brightest*.

 **Try this**

1

> The bus was extremely hot and sticky. Dust particles circulated in the air as we moved along. It was a long and exhausting journey and it seemed to be endless. Despite this, I was happy and contented. Finally, I was no longer seasick and, although worn out, we were buoyed up by the excitement of what was going to happen.

What do the words *buoyed up* mean in the last sentence?   [1 mark]

Tick ✔ **one**.

weary ☐

energised ☐

bobbing along ☐

floating ☐

2

> Aunt Gwen was definitely different! To Jenny, she was evidence that you can be an individual and still have a successful career throughout your life. On the same day that Jenny was 16 and Gwen was 60, they decided to tackle Gwen's photograph album. It was like walking into a paint shop. Aunt Gwen had a different hair colour for every year of her life. One year, emerald green, another, baltic blue. Another year, satsuma orange followed by damson purple. And now, at 60, Gwen had decided to celebrate with a shade of ruby, the symbol for marriage after 40 years. Although the colour hadn't quite turned out to be the shade of ruby she had expected, Gwen was thrilled with the outcome, and Jenny found herself sitting next to a violent shade of red.

*Jenny found herself sitting next to a **violent** shade of red.*

What does the word *violent* mean in the last sentence of this text?   [1 mark]

Tick ✔ **one**.

vicious ☐   brutal ☐   rough ☐   intense ☐

Top tips

- You may be asked to find and copy a word or a group of words from the text.
- You may be asked to replace a word or a group of words either by writing an alternative word or a group of words of your own, or by choosing one from a given list.
- Reread only the part of the text the question refers to. This will save you time.
- Try out all of the words in a given list before choosing which one to use.
- If you are given a list to choose from, some of the words may be trying to trick you – they may be **synonyms** for the original word when it is used in other contexts, but not in this particular context.

Let's practise

From humble beginnings in 2005, the group has produced a remarkable number of 'outside art' projects. 'The Hub', an encampment of five large tepees made from 1500 hubcaps, was exhibited at the Eden Project in 2009.

Find and **copy one** word from the text above that is closest in meaning to *displayed*.

1 Read the question and read it again. What is it asking?

The question is asking you to find an alternative word or group of words for *displayed* without changing the meaning of the sentence.

2 *Displayed* is a verb. Why might you want to display something?

You want other people to look at it.

3 Look for clues that tell you what people may want to look at.

art projects

4 Which piece of art is mentioned?

'The Hub' made out of tepees

5 Read the final sentence about 'The Hub' and replace another word with *displayed* where you think it would not change the meaning of the sentence.

... was displayed at the Eden Project ...

6 Check your answer.

The word is *exhibited*.

Top tips

- Try to think of synonyms for the given word.
- When you think you have found the correct word, replace it with the word given in the question.
- Read the sentence again with the given word in place. It must not alter the meaning of the sentence.
- Read the sentences before and after for clues.

 **Try this**

3

> As food passes through your body, it is broken down into pieces small enough
> to be dissolved in your blood. This process, called digestion, takes place in the
> digestive tract or alimentary canal – a tube that runs from your mouth to a hole
> in your bottom called the anus. Food is broken down physically by chewing
> and churning, and chemically by the action of digestive juices, made by organs
> called glands.
>
> Food is chewed in the mouth and mixed with a digestive juice called saliva,
> which is made in your salivary glands. Saliva moistens the food so it slides down
> your throat easily.

The words *broken down* are used twice in this text. [1 mark]

Which other word or group of words could replace *broken down*?

_____

4

> It was a majestic hall, with wooden towers and pinnacles that reached higher
> than the highest trees. It was the tallest, finest building that had ever been seen
> in the land. And the king was proud of it. Nothing as grand had existed in his
> kingdom before. It became known as the Great Hall.
>
> As soon as the Hall was finished, the party began. It was to be the feast to end
> all feasts. It began one morning as the sun rose and then continued day after
> day, night after night. Long tables sagged under the weight of the food, and
> revellers sagged under the effect of the drink. It made their heads spin and
> caused them to sing louder and louder and to dance more and more wildly.

Find and **copy** the word meaning *partygoers*. [1 mark]

_____

5

> All my earliest memories are very like dreams. I know that none of them are
> proper memories, none that I could really call my own anyway. I feel I've come
> out of half-forgotten, half-remembered times, and I'm sure I've often filled the
> half-forgotten times with made-up memories. Perhaps it's my mind trying to make
> some sense of the unknown. So I can't know for certain where the made-up ones
> end and the real ones begin. All the earliest childhood memories must be like that
> for everyone I suppose, but maybe mine are more blurred than most, and maybe
> that's because I have no family stories to support them, no hard facts, no real
> evidence, no certificates, not a single photograph.

Find and **copy one** word or group of words that shows that the narrator's memories
aren't as clear as they could be. [1 mark]

_____

Explaining words in context

To achieve the expected standard, you need to explain the meaning of words in **context**.

 What you need to know

- Some words or groups of words can mean different things depending on the context in which they are written.
- Quotes from the text can be used to support your answer.
- Questions may require understanding of **synonyms** or **antonyms**.

 Let's practise

One day, my attention was drawn to many insects and some lizards rushing across a bare piece of ground. A little way behind, every stalk and leaf was blackened by ants. The **swarm** divided itself and descended on an old wall. By this means they surrounded many insects; the efforts the poor little creatures made to extricate themselves from such a death were wonderful.

 **Glossary**

- **swarm** collective noun for a group of insects

What does the word *extricate* tell us about the actions of the other insects?

1	Read the question and read it again. What is it asking?	The question is asking you to explain the meaning of *extricate*.
2	What do we know about the other insects? Read around the sentence.	They are surrounded by ants. They don't want to die.
3	In this situation, what might they want to do?	They might try to get out or escape.
4	Write these words in the sentence to see if they make sense.	The efforts the poor little creatures made to escape from such a death were wonderful.
5	Answer the question. Then, check your answer.	*Extricate* tells me that the creatures are trying to escape or get away from the ants.

 Top tips

- Look to see if the definition of the word or the group of words is in the text.
- Pay attention to the words around it. Sometimes, these words will tell you the definition or give you clues about the definition.

 **Try this**

1

14th June. The day she moved away. I could barely stand to read the words. The tear-stained words. As I put down my diary, a new tear began to slowly trickle down my cheek. I couldn't believe she'd been gone for a whole year. My best friend. More importantly, I couldn't believe how much my life had changed since she'd gone. Now, she was coming back. I should be happy but something was niggling at me.

We had so many happy memories together but each time I tried to picture her face, it was blurry. Each time I tried to hear her laugh, it was faint and faded. When I tried to remember the time we spent together, it all sort of smudged into a blot. It seemed **corroded** by time. New memories were invading her space in my mind. I felt so guilty.

Glossary
- **corroded** destroyed or weakened gradually

What does the word *smudged* tell you about the girl's memory of her friend?

[1 mark]

_____

_____

2

While the majority of diagnoses of **myopia** in children used to happen around puberty, increasing numbers of children are needing glasses younger and younger.

And it's children from comfortable backgrounds who are driving this increase. Why? In part, because they are wealthy enough to have access to all those seductive screens and gadgets, says Joanne Hancox, a consultant in **paediatrics** at London's Moorfields Eye Hospital.

Glossary
- **myopia** short-sightedness
- **paediatrics** branch of medicine for babies, children and young people

Why has the word *seductive* been used to describe screens and gadgets?

[1 mark]

_____

_____

3

Eva's report was, as it always was, first rate and outstanding. She had worked hard in her first school and now she was proving to be a big hit too at her new secondary school. Eva liked to show off and brag about her grades. You could never say that Eva or her work was inconspicuous.

The trouble was, Eva was not impressed with her report. She always focused on things she didn't do so well and now she was dwelling on the comment, 'Eva likes music lessons'. To Eva, 'like' wasn't good enough!

Use evidence from the text to explain why *You could never say that Eva or her work was inconspicuous.*

[1 mark]

_____

_____

Retrieving and recording information

To achieve the expected standard, you need to **find** and **record** information in fiction and non-fiction texts.

What you need to know

- Questions may begin with words such as *who, why, what, where, when, how.*
- **Retrieving** information is not a test of memory. The answers will be in the text.

Let's practise

Once again, the **sanctuary** that is Tiggywinkles echoes to the sound of the builders and their mini-monster machines. There is constantly the need to expand our small plot of **rural** Buckinghamshire, to give both the patients and staff modern facilities. We need to reflect the ever-changing experiences of our animals and the staff that care for them.

After open areas were created, a hedgehog enclosure was built to incorporate the hedgehog maternity unit, which the nurses christened 'Hogwarts'.

Now it is time for fences to be renewed to partition eight large hedgehog **recuperation** pens into smaller ones. As the hospital gets busier, every inch of space is crucial. This new hedgehog area will be a welcome addition.

Glossary

- **sanctuary** place of safety
- **rural** countryside
- **recuperation** recovery, usually after an illness or accident

The building work at Tiggywinkles is to improve facilities for patients and staff.

Who are the *patients* and *staff* at Tiggywinkles?

1 Read the question and read it again. What is it asking?

The question is asking you to explain who the patients and staff are at Tiggywinkles.

2 Locate the words in the text. Where are they?

They are in the second sentence.

3 Read on and look for clues.

The following sentence says *our animals and the staff*, so the patients are animals.

4 Read on to find out which animals are patients.

They are hedgehogs.

5 The word *staff* is in the question, so don't repeat it. Find out who they are or what they do by reading ahead.

The next sentence mentions *nurses*.

6 Answer the question using evidence or quote from the text. Then, check your answer.

The patients are hedgehogs and the staff are the nurses who care for them.

Try this

1

Choose your kit carefully. You will need a strong tent, warm sleeping bag and a mat for camping. You should include tools such as a snow shovel and a signalling kit in case you get into difficulties. Travel games will come in handy if bad weather keeps you in your tent! You'll need ski poles and skis or snowshoes to move over snowy terrain. An ice axe and crampons are useful to scale icy slopes. Wearing the right clothing can make the difference between life and death in polar regions. Wearing lots of layers is the key to keeping warm.

Don't skimp on quality when it comes to essentials for a polar trip. Your kit needs to be tough to withstand the harshest conditions on Earth!

According to the text, why should you choose equipment carefully for a trip to the Arctic? [*2 marks*]

Give **two** reasons.

1. _____

2. _____

2

Frogs have been disappearing at an alarming rate in recent decades. Habitat destruction is the main cause of decrease in lowland areas, whereas infectious diseases and climate change cause significant problems for frogs in mountainous regions. Global warming can cause cloud levels to rise in tropical cloud forests. When the clouds rise, the frogs at the newly exposed lower levels lose their habitat as the soil dries, and their eggs can dry up and die. Some frog species live only on a single mountain range, or even on a single mountain, so when problems arise the entire species can easily become extinct.

According to the text, why are frogs *disappearing at an alarming rate*? [*2 marks*]

Give **two** reasons.

1. _____

2. _____

Top tips

- **Skim** the text for a few seconds before you close-read it a second time.
- **Scan** the text and pick out key details.
- Find the information you need and copy it.
- Check that you have answered the correct question (e.g. *who, what, why, when, where, how*).

Let's practise

Hundreds of years ago, the Tower of London was used to hold important prisoners. Only royal prisoners had their heads chopped off there, including Anne Boleyn in 1536 and Catherine Howard in 1542 – both were wives of Henry VIII.

In 1671, Captain Blood attempted to steal the Crown Jewels from the Tower. At this time alligators were kept in the moat, which wasn't drained until 1845.

The Tower became famous for keeping many animals. In 1816, George III was given a grizzly bear to add to the collection.

Unfortunately animals sometimes escaped and attacked people, so the animals were sent to London Zoo in 1832.

Draw lines to match each event to the date it happened.

Event	Date
A grizzly bear lived in the Tower.	1536
Anne Boleyn was beheaded.	1816
Alligators were kept in the moat.	1845
The moat of the Tower was drained.	1671

1 Read the question and read it again. What is it asking?

The question is asking you to match each date to the correct event from the text.

2 Read each of the events and the dates in the question, then find the first date in the text.

It is 1536 and it is in the second sentence.

3 Read the sentence in which it is written to identify the event it refers to.

It refers to Anne Boleyn being beheaded. Draw a line from this event to 1536.

4 Repeat the process for the other dates in the text. Are any unclear?

The sentence containing the date 1671 does not describe any of the events listed in the question.

5 Read the sentence after this one.

The next sentence begins *At this time alligators were kept in the moat*. That is one of the events listed in the question.

6 Have you drawn four lines? What is your answer?

7 Check your answer.

A grizzly bear lived in the Tower.	1536
Anne Boleyn was beheaded.	1816
Alligators were kept in the moat.	1845
The moat of the Tower was drained.	1671

 **Try this**

3

> LEGO building blocks were created by Ole Kirk Christiansen, a Danish man whose company made wooden toys. In 1934 Ole named his business 'LEg GOdt,' which means 'play well' in Danish. In 1947 a special machine was made that could make large quantities of interlocking plastic blocks. By 1949 the new machine was making about 200 different kinds of toys. In 1953, the blocks were called 'LEGO bricks' and, in 1958, a new design meant they looked like the LEGO bricks we know today. In the same year, Godtfred Christiansen became head of LEGO following the death of his father. In the 1960s, LEGO toys were being sold in countries all over the world including the United Kingdom, France and Sweden. By popular demand, other countries soon started selling the toys, including the United States in 1973.

Draw lines to match each LEGO event to the date it happened. [1 mark]

Event		Date
Godtfred Christiansen became head of the LEGO company. •		• 1953
Two hundred kinds of toys were being manufactured. •		• 1958
The company was named LEg GOdt. •		• 1949
Toys were made for the United States. •		• 1934
The bricks were called LEGO bricks. •		• 1973

4

> J.K. Rowling was born on July 31, 1965. She is an international bestselling author, known for the Harry Potter series of books. Her first book, *Harry Potter and the Philosopher's Stone*, was published in 1997. Following the success of this book, Rowling wrote her second book, *Harry Potter and the Chamber of Secrets*, published in 1998. Book three in the series, *Harry Potter and the Prisoner of Azkaban*, followed in 1999 and, in 2000, book four, *Harry Potter and the Goblet of Fire*, became the fastest-selling book in history. The books were translated into many different languages. Rowling continued the series with *Harry Potter and the Order of the Phoenix* in 2003 and, two years later, *Harry Potter and the Half-Blood Prince*. The final book in the series, *Harry Potter and the Deathly Hallows*, was published in 2007.

Draw lines to match each event with the correct date. [1 mark]

Event		Date
Harry Potter and the Order of the Phoenix was published. •		• 2007
The first Harry Potter book was published. •		• 2000
J.K. Rowling was born. •		• 1997
Harry Potter and the Deathly Hallows was released. •		• 2003
The fourth book became the fastest-selling book in history. •		• 1965

Let's practise

> The Mole had been working very hard all the morning, spring-cleaning his little home. First with brooms, then with dusters; then on ladders and steps and chairs, with a brush and a pail of whitewash; till he had dust in his throat and eyes, and splashes of whitewash all over his black fur, and an aching back and weary arms. Spring was moving in the air above and in the earth below and around him, penetrating even his dark and lowly little house with its spirit of divine discontent and longing. It was small wonder, then, that he suddenly flung down his brush on the floor, said 'Bother!' and 'O blow!' and also 'Hang spring-cleaning!' and bolted out of the house without even waiting to put on his coat.

Complete the table about Mole.

What was Mole focused on at the start of the story?	
What time of year was it?	
What did Mole's home look like?	

1 Read the question and read it again. What is it asking?

The question is asking you to complete the table about Mole. The first question is *What was Mole focused on at the start of the story?*

2 Read the text.

The first line in the text says that *Mole had been working hard all morning, spring-cleaning his little home.*

3 What is the second question in the table asking?

What time of year was it?

4 Keep reading until you find where it talks about the time of year. As this could be a date or month, scan for numbers or capital letters but make sure you read the whole sentence.

It says that it was spring.

5 What is the last question asking and where can you find the answer?

It is asking for a description of Mole's home. It is near the end of the text. It can be useful to look for adjectives that might describe his home. It says *his dark and lowly little house.*

6 Check your answers. Do they answer the questions?

Try this

5

Take the whisper of the river,
The thunder of the sea,
The echo of the songbird,
The rustle of the tree,
The howling of the blizzard,
The purring of the cat,
The shudder of the earthquake,
The whistle of the gnat,

The rumble of the storm cloud,
The singing of the sun,
The music of the moonrise,
And mix them one by one,
Till all the notes are silver
And all the chords are gold,
Then give your gift of laughter
To the sick, the sad, the old.

Complete the table using the poem.

[2 marks]

What noise does the blizzard make?	
What does the poem say makes music?	
Who does the poem suggest that you should give your laughter to?	

6

And neither of them stumbled and the candles didn't go out, and at last they came to where they could see a little door in the brick wall on their right. There was no bolt or handle on this side of it, of course, for the door had been made for getting in, not for getting out; but there was a catch (as there often is on the inside of a cupboard door) which they felt sure they would be able to turn.

Both felt that it was becoming very serious, but neither would draw back. Then, with a great shock, they saw that they were looking, not into a deserted attic, but into a **furnished** room. But it seemed empty enough. It was dead silent. Polly's curiosity got the better of her. She blew out her candle and stepped out into the strange room, making no more noise than a mouse.

Glossary

- **furnished** filled with furniture

Using information from the text, put a tick ✔ in the correct box to show whether each statement is **true** or **false**.

[2 marks]

	True	False
They stumbled in the darkness.		
They used the handle to open the little door.		
The looked into a furnished room.		
Polly was very quiet when she stepped into the room.		

Identifying key details

To achieve the expected standard, you need to identify the **key details** in a text.

What you need to know

- Within a text, every paragraph has a key concept or **main idea**. The main ideas in a text are the most important pieces of information the writer wants you to know.
- The **key details** in a text are the words, groups of words or sentences that communicate the main ideas.
- When using key details you can **quote** directly from the text, using inverted commas, or **paraphrase** (use your own words).

Let's practise

Grendel lived in the fens and the foul-smelling marshland beyond the forest. The marsh was littered with oozing pools and the festering remains of dead otters and decaying fish. No one, not even the bravest warrior, went there. The place reeked of evil.

Evil suited Grendel. Half man, half fiend, he was an extraordinary creature with supernatural strength. Covered in a green, horny skin that no sword could cut through, he came from a race of sea monsters, giants, goblins and other outcasts from the human race.

Grendel was in the habit of sleeping for centuries, and he had been asleep so long that the king and his **subjects** had forgotten his existence. If they thought of him at all, they remembered him as a creature from legends. That was their big mistake.

Glossary

- **subject** person living under the rule of a king or queen

Top tips

- Use **skimming** and **scanning** to locate key details that may be repeated within a paragraph or across paragraphs.
- You may be asked to order events from the text, or select the most appropriate summary from a given list.
- Do not include your own **opinion** or add extra information.

The main idea in this text is that Grendel is a *monster*. Give **two** details that support this idea.

1 Read the question and read it again. What is it asking?

The question is asking you to find the key details that support the main idea of the text.

2 How does the writer communicate the idea that Grendel is a monster?

The writer uses descriptive language.

3 Scan the text and look for key details that describe a monster.

lives in foul-smelling marshland; half man, half fiend; green, horny skin; supernatural strength

4 Choose two of the details for the answer. Quote directly from the text if you want to or write the answer in your own words. Then, check your answer.

He is *covered in a green, horny skin*. He is *half man, half fiend*.

 **Try this**

1

> Roald Dahl LOVED chocolate – he had a little red box full of small chocolate bars, which he would bring out every day after dinner. Roald Dahl loved chocolate so much that he started keeping the foil wrappers from all the bars he ate, turning them into a ball. He continued to add to the ball, which stayed on his desk in his writing hut until he died!

According to the text, Roald Dahl *loved chocolate*.
Give **two** key details that support this.

[2 marks]

1. _____

2. _____

2

> When playing some sports, athletes are required to wear special shoes. Two such sports are golf and bowling. Golf shoes have sharp metal spikes called cleats. These cleats help golfers keep their footing while swinging the club. On the other end of the spectrum are bowling shoes, which are very smooth and have almost no traction at all. Bowling shoes help bowlers slide down the lane while throwing the ball. While both of these types of shoes help athletes perform, it is not advisable to wear either of them outside except for sports. Golf shoes and bowling shoes do not have soles that are fit for street use.

Give **one** sentence to **summarise** the main idea in this text.

[1 mark]

_____

_____

Let's practise

The luxurious fashions shown in Elizabethan artwork most often reflect the clothing worn by royalty, the **nobility** and the **elite**.

As in the Middle Ages, the fabrics used to create **garments** for the Elizabethans were wool and linen.

The upper classes wore garments made of silk, satin, velvet, damask and taffeta, in addition to wool and linen.

Finer linens were bleached in the sun, embroidered or block printed. Fashionable decorations included embroidery, lace and gems or pearls sewn onto the fabric.

The fashionable elite used whale bone (baleen) stiffening, willow wood or steel in their **bodices**.

Glossary

- **nobility** upper class
- **elite** privileged
- **garments** clothes
- **bodice** woman's undergarment laced at the front

The paragraphs above describe Elizabethan fashion for rich people.
Find and **copy two** groups of words or sentences to support this.

1 Read the question and read it again. What is it asking?

The question is asking you to find two key details that support the idea that the text is about **rich people's fashions.**

2 Look for other key words that mean rich people across the paragraphs. Use your knowledge of synonyms to help.

Words include *royalty, nobility, elite.*

3 What do the paragraphs tell you about the fashion for these people?

They wore things like silk, satin and taffeta.

4 Look through the other paragraphs for further key details.

Their clothes had decorations that would be expensive. They used whale bone in their bodices.

5 Choose two key words or phrases to support the evidence that the clothing is for rich people. Write each separately.

1 The upper classes wore silk, satin and taffeta.
2 The fashionable elite used whale bone.

6 Check your answer.

 **Try this**

3

Fossils are the **preserved** remains of plants or animals. To be considered fossils, scientists have decided they have to be over 10,000 years old.

First, the body of the animal or plant is usually buried under something soft such as sand or soil. Next, water fills the inside of the body and the soft parts rot away. Finally, the hard parts, such as the skeleton, are left behind.

Over millions of years, the sand and mud build up in layers and eventually turn to rock with the preserved remains of the plant or animal, called a FOSSIL, inside. What was once bone is now rock in the shape of a bone.

Glossary

• **preserved** found in good condition after a long time

[2 marks]

The title of this text is *How Fossils Are Formed*.

Underline two key details from the text that show how fossils are formed.

4

Then, as Miranda fell into a charmed sleep, the source of Prospero's magical **tempest** appeared.

This was Ariel, a strange creature who seemed all made of fire and air, and who was visible only to Prospero. Ariel's special quality was 'to fly,
To swim, to dive into the fire, to ride
On the curled clouds…'

Ariel had been on the island before Prospero arrived, but had been imprisoned in a tree by a witch. He was in pain and misery because it was his very nature to be free, to ride the elements high in the sky, or deep in the earth and below the sea's surface; he could create both roaring storms and healing, soothing music. When Prospero discovered Ariel in the tree he set him free, but on condition he should serve him for twelve years, according to his swift and airy nature.

 **Glossary**

• **tempest** storm

[2 marks]

This narrative describes Prospero's magical helper, Ariel.

Give **two** details to support the idea that Ariel is magical.

1. _____

2. _____

Summarising main ideas

To achieve the expected standard, you need to summarise the **main ideas** in a text.

★ What you need to know

- Within a text, every paragraph has a key concept or main idea. The main ideas in a text are the most important pieces of information the writer wants you to know.

★ Let's practise

In 1947, the *Studebaker Starlight* started a trend for sleek, stylish cars. The following year, a designer working for the Cadillac car company was inspired when a fighter jet flew by. American designers used every trick to make their cars stand out, from stylish fins and shiny chrome bumpers to dazzling paintwork and pointed tail-lights.

Most impressive of all were the stretch limos. Still popular today, they are twice the length of a normal car, with plush leather seats and a drinks bar inside. The rich and famous love to travel by limo. They can soak up the sights in chauffeur-driven luxury, while mirrored windows stop excited fans from seeing in.

What is the main idea in this text? Tick ✔ **one.**

American cars are popular. ☐

American car designs stand out from other cars. ☐

The stretch limo is the most impressive American-designed car. ☐

American car designs are inspired by fighter jets. ☐

1 Read the question and read it again. What is it asking?

The question is asking you to choose one answer that most closely fits the main idea of the text.

2 Read all the choices given. Find evidence in the text that American cars are popular.

The text tells you that the stretch limo is popular. It doesn't mention other popular cars, so discount the first answer choice.

3 Do American cars stand out from others as given in the second choice?

Yes. They have *stylish fins, shiny chrome bumpers, dazzling paintwork and pointed tail-lights*. However, the text does not give any further detail about these features, so it is not the *main* idea of the text.

4 Look at the two choices you have left. Is it possible to eliminate one of them?

The last choice can be eliminated because we only know that one car designer was inspired by a fighter jet.

5 Reread the text to make sure that you are confident the third choice is the main idea of the text. Then tick the correct box.

The main idea is that the stretch limo is the most impressive American car.

6 Check your answer.

Try this

1

Frowning, Jess held her wrist to the moonlight to peer at her watch. Ten minutes had become twenty. So what? It wouldn't feel so long in daylight. It wouldn't feel so long in a crowded noisy bar. Here in the eerie shadows of the ancient temple ruins it was easy to get spooked, that was all.

OK. She was starting to get cross now. *A bit late* didn't mean he had any right to leave her standing here in the darkness. For thirty minutes now!

It wasn't so great in the dark in the shifting moon shadows that made a monster out of every massive tree, a stalking horror out of every unseen animal.

Forty-seven minutes! Time to go.

What is the main idea in this text?　　　　　　　　　　　　　　　　[1 mark]

Tick ✔ one.

The temple was dark and scary.　　　　　□

Jess had been waiting a long time.　　　　□

Jess wanted to leave.　　　　　　　　　　□

Jess had been waiting for a short while.　□

Top tips

• Look for key details in the text that support the question or choices provided.
• Reject answer choices where the clues are absent or limited in the text.
• To be sure you have made the correct choice, read through the text one final time.

Let's practise

> Most of the world's roller coasters are gravity-powered, which means that once a motor has dragged the cars up to the top of the first big hill, it's only the force of gravity that takes you all the way to the end of the ride.
>
> The force that pushes you down into your seat on a roller coaster is called the centripetal force. The need to have enough centripetal force is why a roller coaster's loops aren't circular. Instead, they're what's known as clothoid loops, which look like a circle that someone's squeezed from the sides. As you climb up the loop, you lose speed. In order to keep enough centripetal force to hold you in your seat, you have to tighten up the radius of the loop.

What is the most important thing this text tells you about roller coasters?

1 Read the question and read it again. What is it asking?

The question is asking you to explain the main idea of the text.

2 Are any terms repeated throughout the text?

Yes, *force* – the force of gravity and centripetal force.

3 How does gravity help during the ride?

It keeps the cars going to the end of the ride.

4 How does centripetal force help during the ride?

It keeps you in your seat.

5 Put the information together and answer the question.

Roller coasters use two forces: gravity to keep the ride going and centripetal force to keep you safely in your seat.

6 Check your answer.

Top tips

- Look for key details in the text that relate to the question.
- Identify words or groups of words that are repeated.
- Make the link between key details and repeated words or groups of words.
- Use key details in your answer.

Try this

2

Every day Gabriela followed the **shaman** through the forest and learned about the hundreds of plants he used for medicines; plants to cure earaches and stomach aches, snake and insect bites.

One day Nahtahlah noticed Gabriela scratching her elbow. Going over to a weedee tree, he peeled the bark away. He spread the bright red **sap** on Gabriela's arm. By the next day the fungus and itching had disappeared.

After several months Gabriela left. But every year she returned to Kwamala to learn more and more of the shaman's wisdom.

Glossary

- **shaman** a person who uses ancient healing traditions for cures
- **sap** sugary liquid produced by plants

[1 mark]

What is the most important thing this text tells you about the forest?

_____

_____

3

Robinson spent part of each day sorting his **booty** and storing it away properly in the cave. He also improved his shelter, raising the fence and making a ladder to get in and out, and building a kind of big, wooden porch for the cave entrance with timber from the ship. And in between doing all that, he and Toby explored as much of the island as possible.

'I think we're going to be fine, Toby,' Robinson said as they were heading home late one afternoon. It was the twelfth day since the wreck. 'It's not such a scary place as I thought. There aren't any dangerous wild animals here, just lots of goats, and I can hunt them for meat. I might even be able to catch a few and keep them for their milk. And there are fish in the lagoon, so Freckles and Rufus can have the occasional treat.'

That evening, Robinson sat in his cave surrounded by his supplies in their neat piles, his tools and weapons all neatly arranged too.

Glossary

- **booty** valuable stolen goods

[1 mark]

What is Robinson trying to do?
Explain in **one** sentence.

_____

_____

Making inferences

To achieve the expected standard, you need to make **inferences** from the text.

What you need to know

- Writers often use clues to imply meaning in texts.
- A good reader works like a detective, using these clues to work out missing information. You need to add this information to what you already know in order to make sense of the text.
- Give evidence or use quotes if they support your answer.

Let's practise

I remember the Captain as if it were yesterday, as he came plodding to the inn door, his sea chest following behind in a hand-barrow, a tall, strong, heavy, nut-brown man, his **tarry** pigtail falling over the shoulder of his soiled blue coat, his hands ragged and scarred, with black, broken nails, and the sabre cut across one cheek, a dirty, livid white.

Glossary

- **tarry** coated in tar

What does the Captain's appearance tell you about his character? Give **two** examples.

1	Read the question and read it again. What is it asking?	The question is asking you to infer the Captain's character from the information about his appearance.
2	What does the text tell you about the Captain's appearance?	He is tall with brown skin. His clothes are dirty. His hands are ragged and scarred. He has a scar across his cheek.
3	Do you think this is the usual appearance of a captain?	Captains are usually well dressed and clean.
4	What do the scars tell you?	He has been involved in fights.
5	Answer the question about the Captain's character with evidence from the text.	1. He doesn't care about how he looks because he is dirty. It says his coat is soiled, and his hands are ragged and scarred, with black, broken nails. 2. He is a fighter because he has scars on his cheek and on his hands.
6	Check your answer.	

 **Try this**

1

The dragons thrashed around wildly in the surf, gagging and choking, with their eyes popping, their tails causing such tidal waves that the boys were soaked, even though they were scrambling away from the headland as fast as they could.

Finally, with some last heaving shudders and grim gurgles, both mighty beasts lay still in the water.

There was silence.

The boys stopped running. They stood gasping for breath, watching the motionless beasts with dread. The boys' dragons, which were flying some way ahead of the boys, also turned, and hung still in the air.

Why do you think the boys watched the dragons *with dread*?   [1 mark]

_____

_____

_____

2

One Careful Owner (rumoured to be Queen **Boudicca** of the Iceni)
Low Mileage
Two or Four **Horsepower**
Wheels with Sharp Knives (if required)
5 months Road Tax
Blood-Red Bodywork
inlaid with Roman Bones

Glossary

• **Boudicca** queen of the Celtic Iceni, a tribe living in the East of England before the Roman invasion
• **horsepower** an old-fashioned measurement of power

What impression do you get of the condition of the chariot?   [2 marks]
Give **two** impressions.

1. _____

2. _____

Top tips

• Be a detective. Find clues that help you fill in the missing information.
• Put all the clues together and add them to the information you know.
• Try to **empathise** with a central character. What would you do? How would you feel?
• Use a quote from the text or use your own words to support your answer.

Let's practise

Monday	Tuesday
Polished my scales	Measured my wings
till they shone like the sea.	on the door of the cave
Pity Ma won't let me paint my claws.	still only a measly ten feet long.
Tried trampling the ground –	I'm trying to master
it didn't look bad, but	that flick of the tail
I'm not too happy about my roars.	that knocks a knight down, however strong.

From this poem, you can tell that...

Tick ✔ one.

the narrator is an adult dragon. ☐
the mother is easygoing. ☐
the narrator has a good roar. ☐
the narrator is not confident. ☐

1 Read the question and read it again. What is it asking?

The question is asking you to infer one thing about the poem.

2 Read the poem again. Read all the choices then look at the first choice again. Does the poem tell you who the narrator is?

No. I will need to use inference to answer the question.

3 Gather any clues that tell you the narrator may be an adult dragon.

It does not. It gives clues that it is a young dragon, such as it wants to paint its claws and measure its wings.

4 You can eliminate the first choice. Read on. Is the mother easygoing?

No. She won't let the narrator paint its claws.

5 Does the dragon have a good roar?

No. It is not happy about its roar.

6 Is there any evidence that the dragon is not confident?

It says its wings aren't long enough and that it's trying to master knocking down a knight, which means it can't do it yet.

7 Eliminate the first three choices and tick the last one.

the narrator is not confident.

8 Check you have ticked one box.

 **Try this**

3

Are your children peaky and thin?
Too many late nights? Too much telly?
Forest air and a fattening diet
Will very soon put things right.

A week or two at Sweetmeat Cottage
Is bound to make them scrumptiously chubby.
Children just love my gingerbread house,
My liquorice doors and chimneys.

There's everything here to delight a child,
And one kind lady to see to their needs –
For I love children, tasty little darlings!
Apply without delay.

What are the intentions of the narrator of this poem? Tick ✔ one. [1 mark]

To look after children. ☐

To give parents a break. ☐

To eat children. ☐

To give children a holiday. ☐

4

At first it may seem odd that people would want to live close to a volcano. After all, volcanoes have a nasty habit of exploding, discharging liquid rock, ash, poisonous gases and generally doing things that kill people. Yet, throughout history, people have deliberately chosen to risk all those hazards and live near them, even on the slopes of active volcanoes that have erupted within living memory.

After thousands of years, volcanic rocks become rich in minerals and when they break down they form rich soils. Farmers are able to grow a wide variety of produce including grapes, vegetables, orange and lemon trees and herbs.

The heat from underground steam is used to drive turbines and produce electricity, or to heat water supplies that are then used to provide household heating and hot water. In addition, tourism creates jobs in shops, restaurants, hotels, tourist centres and national parks.

Why do people choose to live near volcanoes? [1 mark]

Tick ✔ one.

Volcanoes are dangerous but attractive. ☐

Fertile soil is created as a result of volcanic eruptions. ☐

People use the liquids and gases from volcanoes. ☐

Houses, roads and buildings can be covered with ash. ☐

Explaining inferences

To achieve the expected standard, you need to explain **inferences** and justify them with evidence from the text.

What you need to know

- Writers often use clues to imply meaning in texts.
- A good reader works like a detective, using these clues to find out missing information. You need to add this information to what you already know in order to make sense of the text.
- Include both the clues and your conclusion in your answer.
- There can be more than one correct answer when explaining **inferences**.

Let's practise

The birds sat on the trees and sang so sweetly that the children used to stop their games in order to listen to them. 'How happy we are here!' they cried to each other.

One day the Giant came back. When he arrived he saw the children playing in the garden.

'What are you doing here?' he cried in a very gruff voice and the children ran away.

'My own garden is my own garden,' said the Giant; 'anyone can understand that, and I will allow nobody to play in it but myself.' So he built a high wall all round it, and put up a notice-board: TRESPASSERS WILL BE PROSECUTED.

What can we infer about the Giant's character? Explain fully, referring to the text in your answer.

1 Read the question and read it again. What is it asking?

The question is asking you to infer the Giant's character, and explain your thoughts.

2 Find clues to tell you about the Giant.

He builds a wall and puts up a notice so the children keep away. He talks to the children in a *gruff* voice.

3 What do these clues tell you?

He is scary, mean and selfish.

4 Answer the question with your ideas and the clues you have found. Then check your answer.

The Giant is selfish and mean because he wants to keep the garden all to himself. He put up a high wall and a sign, and frightened the children away.

Try this

1

> Splat! The coleslaw tub fell right in front of Mum's feet as she opened the fridge door. Splat! Splat! Splat! The butter, milk and leftover lasagne followed quickly behind.
>
> Mum stopped and turned round, her dripping wet coat making even more mess on the floor. She'd arrived just in time to miss the worst of the storm.
>
> What on earth could have happened? It looked like she'd been burgled by a hungry visitor.
>
> She turned around to look at the kitchen bench. Empty pizza boxes, a sharp knife, pools of coke flowing dangerously near the edge. She scooped up a gooey red liquid and tasted it. Mmm! Definitely strawberry doughnut jam; George's favourite. But George was at Scout Camp wasn't he? He wasn't due home until tomorrow morning. Besides, there was far too much food here for one person alone.
>
> Without making a sound, Mum silently inched towards the kitchen door…

What conclusions had Mum come to?   [2 marks]

Give **two** conclusions, referring to the text in your answer.

1. _____

2. _____

2

> Woodland racer
> Acorn chaser
>
> Tree shaker
> Acorn taker
>
> Nut cracker
> Acorn snacker
>
> Sky rider
> Acorn hider
>
> Winter snoozer
> Acorn loser
>
> Spring reminder
> Acorn finder

This poem is called 'Squirrels'.   [2 marks]

Why might this be a good title?

Explain **one** reason, giving evidence from the poem to support your answer.

Reason

_____

Evidence

_____

Top tips

- Ask yourself, 'What did I think about that?', 'What information did I use to think that?' and find clues in the text to support your thinking. You may need to change your original thoughts if the clues to support them aren't there in the text.
- You should answer with as much detail as possible as there may be more marks if you include evidence from the text.

Let's practise

Society's **perception** of clean versus dirty has varied throughout ancient and modern history. In the Elizabethan **era**, it was not **uncommon** for people to bathe fewer than ten times a year. According to written accounts, Elizabeth I declared that she only bathed once a month.

Most people wore the same outfit for days and days in a row. Laundry was done maybe once a year, if at all. Many people wore pomanders, hollow balls filled with dried herbs and flowers, to ward off the smell.

The Elizabethans didn't have toothpaste and weren't very good about cleaning their teeth. Many had rotten teeth and very bad breath. It is said that the reason Elizabeth I never smiled for portraits was because her teeth looked so bad.

Glossary

- **perception** view
- **era** period in history
- **uncommon** unusual

 What does the text tell you about the hygiene of the Elizabethans? Explain your answer fully, referring to the text.

1 Read the question and read it again. What is it asking?

The question is asking you to use information in the text to explain your thoughts on the Elizabethans' cleanliness.

2 Find evidence in the text to tell you what they had to wash.

They had to wash their clothes, bodies and teeth.

3 Did they wash these things often?

They bathed fewer than ten times a year, washed clothes once a year if at all, and weren't good at cleaning teeth.

4 Are these the habits of clean people? What can you infer?

They tell me that they were not clean or didn't care about cleanliness.

5 Put your thoughts together with the evidence. Explain in two or more sentences if you can.

I don't think the Elizabethans were very clean people because they didn't bathe very often. They hardly ever washed their clothes and they had bad teeth, which means that they probably didn't brush them enough.

6 Check your answer.

Try this

3

> **Study maths and science for space jobs, urges astronaut**
>
> An astronaut has called for more children to study maths and science so they are prepared for a future boom in space-related jobs.
>
> James F. Reilly, who completed three space missions and now works for the Kennedy Space Centre, predicted space tourism will become routine and trips to Mars will be possible within the lifetime of today's schoolchildren. To prepare them he said it is vital that they study STEM subjects – science, technology, engineering and maths.
>
> He added that today's schoolchildren should plan to get jobs in space-related industries, rather than computer programming and app development.
>
> Mr Reilly, 61, flew from his home in Colorado to the UK to speak to children and told them it is important that girls take STEM subjects as well as boys.
>
> He said: "My sister is much smarter at maths than me. It is not a gender-limited capability. Don't listen to the culture that says it is a boys' subject."
>
> He added: "Space tourism will be normal within an eight-year-old's lifetime. I think visiting Mars will be possible. It will be like visiting Antarctica is now – an adventure destination."

Explain why studying STEM subjects is vital for the future. [2 marks]

_____

_____

4

> But it was Joey Father loved best. If ever he got sick, Father would bed down with him in his stable and never leave his side. He loved that horse like a brother, more maybe. Anyway, one day, a few months after the war started, Father goes off to market to sell some fat sheep. In them days of course, you had to drive them down the road to market. No lorries, nothing like that. So he was gone most of the day. Meanwhile the army's come to the village looking for good sturdy horses, and they're paying good money too. They needed all the horses they could get for the cavalry, for pulling the guns maybe, or the ammunition wagons, ambulances too. Most things were horse-drawn in them days. Father comes back from market, and sees Joey being taken away. It's too late to stop it. It was his own father that did it. He'd gone and sold Joey to the army for forty pounds.

Explain how Father might have felt when he discovered his horse had been sold. [2 marks]

Explain **one** way, giving evidence from the text to support your answer.

_____

_____

_____

Predicting

To achieve the expected standard, you need to **predict** what might happen next in a text.

What you need to know

- Sometimes information in a text is stated outright and sometimes it is implied.
- Good readers use clues in the text to explain what might happen next.
- **Prediction** questions are usually based on fiction texts.
- Your answers should refer to the plot, characters or events that have happened.
- Your answers should be written with detail, in one or two sentences, supported by evidence from the text.

Let's practise

Grendel hated the music. He hated it because he hated the humans that made it. He hated it with a hatred that burnt bright as a star. He hated it as only a demon can hate. It reminded him of what an outcast he was. In his ears, that music sounded like the buzzing of flies.

Why should people be happy, he wondered. Why should they make music and sing and hold great feasts while he sat alone in a stinking bog? He was full of jealousy and hatred. The king had left his favourite warriors to guard the Hall, but because there was peace in the land they did not take their guard duty seriously. They fell asleep, and did not hear Grendel croaking his terrible song as he moved out from the shadows towards them:

'Sweet human meat's the best to eat,

And human bones the best to grind.'

What might Grendel do when he arrives at the Hall? Explain fully, referring to the text in your answer.

1 Read the question and read it again. What is it asking?

The question is asking you to use the information in the text to make a prediction about Grendel's actions.

2 Look for previous clues to tell you what Grendel is like.

He hates music. He is full of jealousy and hatred. He likes to eat human meat.

3 How does this make you feel?

I feel frightened and worried that something bad will happen at the Hall.

36

4 | Ask yourself, 'What is happening at the Hall right now?' | **The guards are on duty but they are asleep.**

 5 | Link the clues together to predict what might happen next. Use evidence from the text or direct quotes to support your answer. | **Grendel might kill the sleeping guards and eat them because in his song it says *Sweet human meat's the best to eat*.**

6 | Check your answer.

Try this

1

> Autumn has merely just arrived and the competition has already begun
> To clear the leaves through nature and not by the hands of man.
> So mesmerising to look at the leaves, as some simultaneously depart,
> A sudden wind blew with a loud noise, and I thought that one had a head start.
>
> One by one, the leaves kept falling and most gently hit the ground.
> 'Oops,' that was just an accident, one landed and twisted around,
> Gyrating through the branches, this leaf kept 'starring' at me,
> Other leaves saw how it was distracted and tried to overtake, unnoticeably.
>
> Hey, there is no competition in nature, that is the way it is meant to be,
> Wait for a few seasons and guess what appears again on every tree.
> What was once so fully laden now almost looks so bare.
> Don't be so surprised by this event, it happens every year.

Look at the last verse.   *[1 mark]*

Explain what might happen next year.

_____

_____

_____

Top tips

- There will be clues in the text. Go back and look for them.
- Identify how characters behave, or how events unfold.
- Do not make up information or clues and do not answer with information that is not relevant to the text.
- Refer to key elements of plot, character or information in your answer.

Understanding texts

To achieve the expected standard, you need to find information and explain how it links to the meaning of the whole text.

What you need to know

- Every piece of information given contributes to the meaning of the whole text.
- The meaning of the text is what it is telling you.

Let's practise

> Menorca is one of the Balearic Islands located in the Mediterranean Sea belonging to Spain. The name 'Menorca' actually means 'windy island'. Menorca is the first place in Spain to see sunrise each day and has over 300 sunny days every year. It has more than 100 sandy beaches and it has beautiful crystal clear waters. The island is home to around 99,000 people and they host over 1 million visitors every year.

> Why do so many people visit Menorca each year?
> Give **two** reasons.

1 Read the question and read it again. What is it asking?	The question is asking you to say why lots of people visit Menorca.
2 Read the text again and look for something a visitor to the island would like.	It is located in the Mediterranean Sea.
3 Continue reading the whole passage to find something that would really attract so many people.	It has lots of sunny days every year, which would be nice.
4 Write this answer down.	lots of sunny days
5 Read the text again and find another reason.	There are lots of sandy beaches and clear water.
6 Choose one of your facts and write a second answer. Then, check your answers.	sandy beaches

Try this

1

> It was the best day ever! I went with my children, both boys, aged 10 and 13, and there was so much for both of them to do!
>
> We had an amazing time. My children want to go every weekend!
>
> My youngest loves animals. He adored the zoo and the petting farm. It's a must for younger children and animal lovers.
>
> My eldest and his friends love the rides. They've been time and time again. The rides are fantastic. They love it!

According to the text, what makes the zoo an amazing place? [2 marks]
Give **two** reasons.

1. _____

2. _____

2

> There is more than one way to have a successful school day, but a great way is to be well prepared. The first thing you should do is complete your homework the night before. Don't try to do your work in the morning, it will be too stressful and you may not have enough time. Next, you need to go to bed at a reasonable time. If you stay up too late, you will not be able to focus in class and you may even fall asleep. Lastly, you should wake up early. This will give you time to get ready and feel good about yourself, and you'll also be able to get something to eat before the day begins. So remember, one way to have a successful school day is to do your homework the night before, go to bed early, and wake up early. Have a great day!

Identify **two** ways the text says you can help yourself have a successful [2 marks]
school day.

1. _____

2. _____

Top tips

- Read the whole of the text again before selecting an answer.
- Once you have found one answer check that this answers the question.
- Read through the passage again to find the second answer.
- Check you have written two different answers on each line.

Let's practise

Where do we find Hiccup at the start of the film?
In this film there's more adventure and more challenges. Now everyone in Berk, even Hiccup's father, old Stoick, has a dragon. But Hiccup is dealing with the obligations of manhood, which are starting to pile up.

We meet some extraordinary new dragons in the film. Can you say anything about the Alpha, the creature at the top of the dragon hierarchy?
The Alpha is the king of all dragons and it's massive. What's cool is that instead of breathing fire like most dragons, it breathes ice and is pretty amazing.

What can you tell us about the plot and Hiccup's journey this time around?
Hiccup finds out that there is someone else who has the ability to control dragons. It turns out it is his mother, Valka, who he has not seen since he was a baby. He meets her, and his dad Stoick is reconnected with his long-lost love, the woman he thought was gone forever.

Find and **copy** the group of words that tells you that Hiccup has new responsibilities now he is growing up.

1 Read the question and read it again. What is it asking?

The question is asking you to find the words that tell us that Hiccup has new responsibilities now he is growing up.

2 Read the text and find where he talks about Hiccup's responsibilities.

It is in the answer to the first interview question, where he talks about obligations.

3 What about the 'now he is growing up' part of the question?

That is a reference to his manhood.

4 So, what is the group of words you need to copy?

obligations of manhood

5 Remember to check that you haven't copied any extra words.

 **Try this**

3

When a river receives a lot of extra water it may flood. During a flood there is plenty of water, and most people wouldn't think that dehydration was a serious risk, but flood waters are mostly polluted and not safe to drink. People who drink the contaminated water may suffer from illnesses or diseases such as **typhoid**. You can prepare for flooding by filling many containers with fresh, clean drinking water. You can also use sandbags to protect your house and to soak up the water. Be prepared and be safe.

Glossary
- **typhoid** a disease that causes a fever

What does the text say is the surprising risk to humans when rivers flood? [1 mark]

Tick ✔ **one**.

pollution ☐

dehydration ☐

contamination ☐

flooding ☐

4

Your heart is a muscular organ, which, unlike other muscles, never gets tired.

Your heart is located a little to the left of the middle of your chest, and it's about the size of your fist. The heart muscle is special because of what it does.

The heart acts like a pump because it transports blood around your body. The blood provides your body with the oxygen and **nutrients** it needs. It also carries away waste.

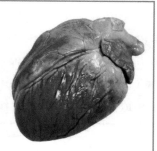

Your heart is divided into four parts called chambers. The two upper chambers are called atria. They are joined to two lower chambers, called ventricles. The right side of your heart receives blood from the body and pumps it to the lungs. The left side of the heart does the exact opposite: it receives blood from the lungs and pumps it out to the body.

Glossary
- **nutrients** things that are needed for life

Find and **copy** the group of words that tells you what makes the heart such a special muscle. [1 mark]

_____

Understanding fiction

To achieve the expected standard, you need to find and explain how narrative content is related and contributes to meaning as a whole.

What you need to know

- Everything that happens within a text helps to contribute to its meaning.
- In non-fiction, this is focussed on sections that give information, summarise the key points, give a contrasting viewpoint, highlight important information or engage the reader.
- In fiction texts, different parts of a story can introduce the setting, discuss past events, describe the action or focus on the moral of the story.
- You need to be able to identify the purpose of each section of a text as well as the whole text.
- This section will focus on narrative.

Let's practise

Suddenly he – the captain, that is – began to pipe up his eternal song:

'Fifteen men on the dead man's chest –

Yo-ho-ho, and a bottle of rum!

Drink and the devil had done for the rest –

Yo-ho-ho, and a bottle of rum!'

At first I had supposed 'the dead man's chest' to be that identical big box of his upstairs in the front room, and the thought had been mingled in my nightmares with that of the one-legged seafaring man.

Draw lines to match each section to its main content.

Section	Main content
Suddenly he – the captain – began to pipe his eternal song:	Quotation highlighting what they are singing
Fifteen men on the dead man's chest – Yo-ho-ho, and a bottle of rum! *Drink and the devil had done for the rest – Yo-ho-ho, and a bottle of rum!*	First-hand thoughts and feelings from the character
At first I had supposed 'the dead man's chest' to be that identical big box of his upstairs in the front room, and the thought had been mingled in my nightmares with that of the one-legged seafaring man.	Introduction to the song

1 Read the question and read it again. What is it asking?

The question is asking you to match each section to its main content.

2 What clues will help you to identify the quotations used for what they are singing?

The song is in inverted commas and quotes the words for the song.

3 What clues will help you to identify the first-hand thoughts and feelings from the character?

The text uses the first person 'I' and it mentions that he thought that the dead man's chest had been mingled in his nightmares.

4 What clues will help you to identify the introduction to the song?

The song is introduced using a colon.

5 Draw lines to the correct answers.

6 Check your answer.

Try this

1

I had to do it. Just this once. Mr Adams was not going to hurt Ella any more.

He'd worked his way through the class. I'd been punished more than once and I knew just how it felt. As he raised his hand, I knew I had to protect my sister. I leaped onto his arm. Mr Adams stumbled against the wooden desk and fell backwards as Ella cowered in the corner.

'Leave her alone,' I cried. 'You're a bully, you know that?' I shouted, secretly quivering inside. A noise behind me told me that the rest of the class were standing up, beating their desks with their fists and cheering.

a) Which of the following would be the most suitable summary of this text?

Tick ✔ one.

Classroom learning ☐

Classroom dreams ☐

Helping your sister ☐

Bullying pupils ☐

b) Draw lines to match each section to its main content.

[2 marks]

Section

'Leave her alone,' I cried. 'You're a bully, you know that?'

A noise behind me told me that the rest of the class were standing up, beating their desks with their fists and cheering.

I knew just how it felt. As he raised his hand, I knew I had to protect my sister. I leaped onto his arm. Mr Adams stumbled against the wooden desk and fell backwards as Ella cowered in the corner.

I had to do it. Just this once. Mr Adams was not going to hurt Ella any more.

Main content

Reactions from the other characters

Key actions

Introduction to the section

Direct speech explaining what the character said

★ **Top tips**

- Read the question carefully.
- If it asks you to draw lines, make sure your lines are clear.
- If you make a mistake, ensure that your new answer is very clear.
- Do not draw lines to more than one answer.

Let's practise

Act 1, Scene 1. A deserted place
Enter three witches.

First witch:	When shall we three meet again?
	In thunder, lightning or in rain?
Second witch:	When the **hurly-burly's** done.
	When the battle's lost and won.
First witch:	Where the place?
Second witch:	Upon the **heath**.
Third witch:	There to meet with Macbeth.
All:	Fair is foul and foul is fair.
	Hover through the fog
	and filthy air!
Exit	

Glossary

- **hurly-burly** confusion/chaos
- **heath** moorland

What is the purpose of this playscript?

Tick ✔ one.

to summarise	☐
to entertain	☐
to inform	☐
to contrast events	☐

1 Read the question and read it again. What is it asking?

The question is asking you to identify the purpose of the text.

2 What type of text is it?

It is a playscript and it is about the three witches from the text 'Macbeth'.

3 Why do we have a playscript?

It is the words for characters to say in a play to be performed for an audience. It normally entertains the audience.

4 Could there be any other answers?

No. It is not summarising the events, giving information like a non-fiction text or contrasting (comparing) events.

5 Tick the box that says 'to entertain'.

6 Check your answer and all possible answers.

Try this

2

> 'My wish is that everything I touch will turn to gold,' he ordered. 'I want my furniture to be gold, I want my clothes to be made of gold, I want my palace to be golden.'
>
> The god Dionysus listened to Midas and immediately granted his wish.
>
> The beautiful flowers in Midas' garden turned to gold when Midas approached and touched them. The king grew hungry and thin, for each time he tried to eat, he found that his meal had turned to gold. His water, his bed, his clothes, his friends, and eventually the whole palace were turned to gold.

'My wish is that everything I touch will turn to gold,'

What is the purpose of this section of the text?

[1 mark]

Tick ✔ **one.**

actions ☐   past events ☐

dialogue ☐   setting ☐

3

> The serpent slithered slowly down, asking Eve if she would like to eat an apple from the Tree of Knowledge. 'I can only eat fruit that does not grow on the Tree of Knowledge. If we eat that, we die.'
>
> 'But you will not die,' said the serpent. 'You know you really want to eat one.
>
> 'Look at how delicious it looks. It's only an apple.'
>
> Eve gazed at the Tree and at the juicy fruit. It looked delicious and she was hungry. Surely one wouldn't hurt. Perhaps the serpent was right. She knew she shouldn't. She'd promised she wouldn't, but surely one wouldn't hurt. Eve quickly picked an apple and bit into it.

What is the purpose of this section of the text?

[1 mark]

Tick ✔ **one.**

to introduce the setting ☐

to share a lesson ☐

to show key actions and events ☐

to summarise key information ☐

Identifying and explaining language choices

To achieve the expected standard, you need to identify and explain how the choice of language enhances the meaning of texts.

★ What you need to know

- Writers use language in different ways to keep readers interested.
- Writers use **imagery** to produce vivid images in a reader's mind and to encourage readers to connect with texts, to increase enjoyment and develop thinking skills.
- Vivid images can be created through the use of interesting words and descriptions.
- **Figurative language** can also be used. This is language that has a different meaning from the literal or 'usual' meaning. Examples include **simile**, **metaphor**, **alliteration**, **onomatopoeia** and **personification**.
- The use of figurative language and vivid descriptions will normally be referred to as 'descriptions' in the test.

★ Let's practise

The reindeer were about the size of Shetland ponies and their hair was so white that even the snow hardly looked white compared with them; their branching horns were **gilded** and shone like something on fire when the sunrise caught them. Their harness was of scarlet leather and covered with bells.

★ Glossary
- **gilded** covered with gold

… shone like something on fire when the sunrise caught them.

What does this description suggest about the reindeer's horns?

1 Read the question and read it again. What is it asking?	The question is asking you to explain what … *shone like something on fire when the sunrise caught them* means.
2 What have the reindeer's horns been compared to?	It says their horns shine like *something on fire* when the sunrise catches them.
3 Ensure you do not repeat the same words in your answer.	It says *like something on fire* but I will not use this in my answer.
4 What does this comparison suggest about the reindeer's horns?	
5 Check your answer.	It suggests that the horns are beaming and glow brightly in the sun.

Try this

1

> In the clearing, the piglets snuffled with no regard to the danger that was lurking nearby. They forgot to look up from the forest floor as they foraged deep into the warmth of the fetid, damp soil, rotten with decaying leaves and berries.
>
> Without warning, the weary wolf entered the clearing without making a sound. Watching from a close distance, he waited patiently. It wasn't time yet!

… the weary wolf entered the clearing without making a sound.
What does the word *weary* tell you about the wolf?

[1 mark]

_____

_____

2

> A rainbow is a painted smile
> turned upside down.
> It's a multi-coloured bridge
> spanning the streets of town.
>
> A rainbow is a brilliant band
> across my sister's hair.
> It's a fluorescent mountain
> Piercing the morning air.

What is the rainbow being compared to in this poem?

[3 marks]

Give three different things.

1. _____

2. _____

3. _____

3

> Great is the sun, and wide he goes
> Through empty heaven with **repose**;
> And in the blue and glowing days
> More thick than rain he showers his rays.

Glossary

- **repose** state of rest

Find and **copy** a group of words that is closest in meaning to *spreads out.*

[1 mark]

_____

Top tips

- Look for how ideas or objects are compared using words such as *like* or *as*.
- Identify ways in which objects have been given human qualities. Think about what this means and how it enhances meaning.
- Identify ways in which ideas or objects with similar characteristics are compared to each other.
- Remember to use evidence from the text, where appropriate.
- Name the **language feature** in your answer if this is relevant.

Let's practise

> Her face was white – not merely pale, but white like snow or paper or icing-sugar, except for her very red mouth. It was a beautiful face in other respects, but proud and cold and stern.

> *... like snow or paper or icing-sugar,*
>
> What does this description suggest about the girl's face?

1 Read the question and read it again. What is it asking?

The question is asking you to explain what ... *like snow or paper or icing-sugar*, means.

2 What has the girl's face been compared to?

It is comparing the colour of her face to snow, paper or icing-sugar.

3 Ensure you do not repeat the same words in your answer.

It says *pale like snow*, etc. but I will not use this in my answer.

4 What does this comparison suggest about the girl's face?

It suggests that her face was extremely pale – whiter than white.

5 Check your answer and ensure it makes sense.

Try this

4

> The night is a big black cat
> The moon is her topaz eye,
> The stars are the mice she hunts at night
> In the field of the sultry sky.

The night is a big black cat.

What does this description tell you about how the night looked?

[1 mark]

_____

_____

5

> Round one month, oval another.
> Squashed and without air, begging to be filled again.
> White and grey marks from being kicked about and used
> on the football pitch, up in the vast expanse of space.
> The moon, just waiting to be used, waiting to make its first, victorious goal.
> Speckled sparkling spectators look on.

What is the moon being compared to?

[1 mark]

Tick ✔ one.

a football pitch ☐

a spectator ☐

an oval ☐

a football ☐

6

> The salmon with a hat on was conducting with a baton
> And it tried to tune the tuna fish by playing on its scales.
> The scales had all been flattened when the tuna fish was sat on
> on purpose by a porpoise and a school of killer whales.
> So the salmon with the hat on fiddled with his baton
> while the angelfish got ready to play the tambourine.

What have the salmon's actions been compared to?

[1 mark]

Tick ✔ one.

playing a tuna fish ☐

conducting music ☐

singing a song ☐

fiddling a violin ☐

Explaining how language choices enhance meaning

To achieve the expected standard, you need to explain how the language choices a writer makes enhance the meaning of a text.

What you need to know

- You need to show you understand what the writer intended to do.
- Writers enhance the meaning of texts through their choice of language. Effective language choices help readers connect with texts, increase enjoyment, develop thinking skills and influence the reader's imagination and emotions.

Let's practise

There was silence for a split second and then the **bombardment** commenced. The low rumbles and booms of the shells making contact with the ground echoed in the distance. Sharp cracks and blasts of rifle fire filled the air, shattering the silence into tiny shards.

Glossary

- **bombardment** a continuous attack with bombs and other missiles

… rumbles and booms … cracks and blasts.
What do these sounds suggest about what it was like during the war?

1	Read the question and read it again. What is it asking?	The question is asking you to explain what the sounds *rumbles, booms, cracks* and *blasts* suggest about the battle.
2	What do these words suggest about the battle?	They create the sense that the noises were loud and frightening. It's giving you a sense of the atmosphere.
3	Write your answer, explaining what the words mean.	The descriptions show how loud and frightening it would be to experience a war.
4	Check your answer and ensure it makes sense.	

 **Try this**

1

> His giant iron head, shaped like a dustbin, but as big as a bedroom, slowly turned to the right, slowly turned to the left. His iron ears turned, this way, that way. He was hearing the sea. His eyes, like headlamps, glowed white, then red, then infra-red, searching the sea. Never before had the Iron Man seen the sea.

a) *His giant iron head …*

What does this description suggest about the giant's head?　　　[1 mark]

_____

b) *His eyes, like headlamps, …*

What does this description suggest about the giant's eyes?　　　[1 mark]

_____

2

> George loves ginger nuts at school whilst playing games
> Harry's hunger never ceases especially on a plane
> Poppy picks purple plums while poking at her peas
> Jack eats juicy jelly while jigging to a beat
> Sophia slurps sloppy soup, sitting in the sand
> Betty burps borlotti beans, dancing to the band.

Find and **copy** a group of words which means *that does not come to an end.*　　　[1 mark]

_____

3

> It was a genie. No doubt about it. He was no taller than her pencil and mist still curled around him; but he looked like every genie she had ever seen in books: a little fat belly, with a silk bodice and billowing **pantaloons** that looked for all the world as if they had been woven from silver shifting mists. Tiny stars winked all over them and they were held up by a belt of pure gold. On his feet were the tiniest curly slippers, with pointed ends.

**Glossary**

- **pantaloons** baggy trousers fastened just above the ankle

Give **two** different descriptions of what the genie looks like.　　　[2 marks]

1. _____

2. _____

4

> CRRRAAAASSSSSSSH!
> Down the cliff the Iron Man came toppling, head over heels.
> CRASH!
> CRASH!
> CRASH!
> From rock to rock, snag to snag, tumbling slowly.
> And as he crashed and crashed and crashed, his iron legs fell off.

According to the text, the Iron Man *crashed and crashed and crashed*.   [1 mark]

What does this suggest about his journey down the cliff?

_____

5

> 'There's a boy down the road who got some superglue on his finger without knowing it and then he put his finger to his nose.' Mr Wormwood jumped. 'What happened to him?' he spluttered. 'The finger got stuck inside his nose,' Matilda said, 'and he had to go around like that for a week. People kept saying to him, "Stop picking your nose," and he couldn't do anything about it.'
>
> 'Serve him right,' Mrs Wormwood said. 'He shouldn't have put his finger up there in the first place. It's a nasty habit. If all children had superglue put on their fingers they'd soon stop doing it.'
>
> Matilda said, 'Grown-ups do it too, Mummy. I saw you doing it yesterday in the kitchen.'

What does the word *spluttered* tell us about how Mr Wormwood felt?   [1 mark]

_____

Top tips

- Refer to an example in the text if you are asked for it.
- Describe how the language feature has an impact on the reader and enhances meaning, for example by building a better picture or changing their emotions.
- Include two or more explanations in your answer. You may achieve an additional mark for each explanation.

6

George opened his eyes and sat upright in bed. He ruffled his curly hair and in his confused state tried to make sense of the layout of his room. After a stifled yawn, it dawned on him that today was the day. The clock told him he was late. They were due to leave in fifteen minutes. George had been promised a new puppy and he was going to choose it with his dad that morning. He couldn't wait! With athletic grace, he leaped out of bed, flung back the curtains and skipped over to a pile of crumpled clothes. He couldn't get them on quick enough! As he put one leg in his trousers, George toppled over onto the bed.

How does the language in the text make the reader feel?   [1 mark]

Tick ✔ one.

confused   ☐

sad   ☐

excited   ☐

jealous   ☐

7

In the hamlet not a soul was visible. The buildings were like dead buildings. Their two voices rose and fell as in a dead world. The two servants, the three dogs, were without movement. Suddenly, and for no apparent reason, Irvine's servant struck a **flint** and threw, with a careless gesture, some lighted fragment on to the straw-covered floor of the **mean** barn that was just beyond the wall of the house. The flame ran along the floor and very quickly caught the bare rafters.

Glossary
- **flint** a rock used to light a fire
- **mean** broken-down

Find and **copy** a group of words that could make the reader feel scared.   [1 mark]

_____

Making comparisons

To achieve the expected standard, you need to make **comparisons** in a text.

★ What you need to know

- Making **comparisons** is about showing how information, characters or events in the text are similar or different.
- All the texts will be non-fiction.

★ Let's practise

They may have a fearsome reputation, but those terrifying meat-eating dinosaurs we see in the movies may have had a softer side. Some were so gentle, they were used as babysitters, according to new research. And they'd have had a big job on their hands as some trusted **juveniles** would have been in charge of dozens of babies while their parents were out looking for food. Rather than seeing the babies as a potential dinner, the older juvenile may well have been a big brother or sister helping care for its younger siblings.

★ Glossary

- **juvenile** young adult

What is different about the babysitter dinosaurs compared with the other dinosaurs? Give **two** examples.

1	Read the question and read it again. What is it asking?	The question is asking you to state two differences between the babysitter dinosaurs and other dinosaurs.
2	Locate the description of other dinosaurs throughout the text.	*terrifying, meat-eating, fearsome*
3	Locate the description of the babysitter dinosaurs.	*softer, gentle, trusted*
4	What did the parents do while the babysitters were in charge?	They were hunting for food.
5	Use the information you have gathered to compare the two types of dinosaurs. Then, check your answer.	Babysitter dinosaurs looked after the young ones. The other dinosaurs hunted for food. Babysitter dinosaurs were gentle and caring. The other dinosaurs were fearsome.

Try this

1

> Sparklers and smoke bombs are my favourite kinds of fireworks. They are both fun but they are also quite different. After you light a smoke bomb, you should put it on the ground and run. Stand back and watch it go! When you light a sparkler, however, you continue to hold it until it has finished sparkling. You wave your hand around and have a great time making patterns in the dark! They also burn differently. Sparklers create bright lights and sparks when you light them, but smoke bombs create smoke in different colours. Remember: smoke bombs and sparklers are both extremely dangerous and should only be used by professionals, or supervised by an adult.

Explain **two** ways sparklers are different to smoke bombs.   [2 marks]

1. _____

2. _____

2

>  A recent article has blamed humans for the sudden decline in UK butterflies, bees and beetles. It identified that the human population has increased rapidly: it has nearly doubled in the last 35 years. The decline in the insect population has primarily been due to the loss of their habitat because of increased human activity. As a result, the number of these creepy-crawlies has dropped by nearly 60%. You might think that this isn't a problem but actually they help us by pollinating our food crops. They are also food for other animals who might now struggle to find enough to eat.

How does the change in the number of humans on Earth compare with the change in the number of insects?   [2 marks]

_____

_____

Top tips

- Words to show that the text is comparing and contrasting more than one thing may include: *like, unlike, but, even though, while, however, although.*
- Questions may require you to compare one part of a text with another part of the same text.
- You will be expected to give the similarities or the differences in your answer.

Let's practise

Chocolate Crispy Cakes

Ingredients

75 g / 3 oz plain chocolate

150 g / 5 oz butter chopped,
plus extra for greasing

100 g / 3½ oz puffed rice cereal

Method

First, you will need to grease a rectangular dish so that the cakes do not stick. Next, chop the chocolate into chunks and carefully place with the butter in a pan and melt. After that, add the puffed rice cereal to the melted mixture and stir. Finally, press the mixture firmly into the dish and chill overnight.

Chocolate Crispy Cakes

Ingredients

75 g / 3 oz plain chocolate

150 g / 5 oz butter chopped,
plus extra for greasing

100 g / 3½ oz puffed rice cereal

Method

1 Grease a rectangular dish.
2 Chop the chocolate into chunks.
3 Place the chunks in a pan with butter. Melt.
4 Add puffed rice cereal to melted mixture.
5 Press the mixture firmly into dish.
6 Chill overnight.

> What is different about the way the method is written in the two texts?

1 Read the question and read it again. What is it asking?

The question is asking you to compare the way in which the two methods are written.

2 How is the first method written?

It uses time connectives: *first, next, after* and *finally.*

3 How is the second method written?

It uses numbered steps.

4 Answer the question saying how the first method is different compared to the second.

The difference is that the first method is written using time connectives, and the second is written using numbered steps.

5 Check your answer.

 **Try this**

3

a) Attention all students! Attention all kids!
   Hold onto your horses! Hold onto your lids!
   We have just exactly the thing that you need
   whenever you've way too much homework to read.

   The Marvellous Homework & Housework Machine
   will always make sure that your bedroom is clean.
   It loves to write book reports ten pages long,
   then put all your toys away where they belong.

b) Who's been at the toothpaste?
   I know some of you do it right
   And you squeeze it right from the bottom
   and you roll the tube up from the bottom when it gets used up don't you?

   But somebody, somebody here – you know who you are,
   you dig your thumb in, anywhere, anyhow,
   and you've turned that tube of toothpaste into a squashed sock

Give **one** way in which the first poem is different to the second poem.   [1 mark]

_____

_____

4

During the summer, parents are often looking for exciting places to go, and things to do to entertain their children close to home, that won't cost a fortune. Libraries are a useful resource. They often provide free book trails or challenges, invite authors to read, and hold dressing up sessions for younger children. Local community groups regularly provide sports and arts and craft activities at reduced costs or for a small donation.

Looking for something interesting to do with your children this holiday? If you are willing to look further afield, and spend a little money to keep your children entertained, trips to the theatre, theme parks and popular museums offer endless opportunities to distract and amuse children of all ages. Child-friendly activity centres provide a wide range of outdoor activities from canoeing and abseiling to archery and climbing. Children can visit on a daily basis or stay, *parent free*, overnight! Although slightly more expensive, these mini breaks do provide the opportunity for children to become independent and make a new set of friends.

Write **one** thing that is different about the places close to home compared with those further afield.   [2 marks]

_____

_____

Glossary

Alliteration A series of words in which the same sound is repeated.

Antonym A word that is the opposite of another.

Comparisons Making the link between two similar things.

Context Background information to make the meaning clearer.

Empathise To put yourself in the situation of someone else.

Figurative language Words whose meaning is different from the usual meaning.

Imagery Using words to allow the reader to paint images in their imagination.

Inference A conclusion reached on the basis of reasoning and evidence.

Key details Specific information that contributes to the main idea in a piece of writing.

Language features The ways in which writers communicate meaning through word choice and sentence structure.

Main idea The most important piece of information the writer wants you to know.

Metaphor When one object is described as another: *the sun is a golden apple*.

Onomatopoeia Language imitating the sound of an object or action.

Opinion A view about something, not necessarily based on fact or knowledge.

Paraphrase To reword something written or spoken using different words.

Personification Language giving human qualities to an animal or an object.

Prediction Working out what will happen next using the information you are given.

Quote To repeat or copy words from the text.

Retrieve To find something in a text (usually information).

Scan To search for specific information.

Simile A way to compare one thing to another using the words 'like' or 'as'.

Skim To read quickly to note the important points.

Summarise To give a brief statement of the main points.

Synonym A word that has the same, or very similar, meaning to another word.

Answers

Note: *Answers provided are suggestions. Always use professional judgement when considering children's responses.*

Understanding words in context (pages 9, 11)
1 tick: energised
2 tick: intense
3 broken up; disintegrated
4 revellers
5 half-forgotten, half-remembered times; made-up memories; blurred

Explaining words in context (page 13)
1 The memories aren't clear / are muddled together / are fading. They have deteriorated over time.
2 They are really tempting. / They are attractive. / You can't stop playing on them.
3 Eva liked to be noticed, she liked to 'show off and brag about her grades'.

Retrieving and recording information (pages 15, 17, 19)
1 Award 1 mark each for any two of the following: warmth; shelter; in case you get into difficulties; entertain yourself; withstand harshest conditions on Earth.
2 Award 1 mark each for habitat destruction; global warming.
3 Godtfred Christiansen became head of the LEGO company.   1958
  Two hundred kinds of toys were being manufactured.   1949
  The company was named LEg GOdt.   1934
  Toys were made for the United States.   1973
  The bricks were called LEGO bricks.   1953
4 *Harry Potter and the Order of the Phoenix* was published.   2003
  The first Harry Potter book was published.   1997
  J.K. Rowling was born.   1965
  Harry Potter and the Deathly Hallows was released.   2007
  The fourth book became the fastest-selling book in history.   2000

5

What noise does the blizzard make?	howling
What does the poem say makes music?	The moonrise
Who does the poem suggest that you should give your laughter to?	To the sick, the sad and the old.

2 marks for all three answers correct, 1 mark for two answers correct.
6 Award 1 mark for three correct or 2 marks for all four correct: false, false, true, true

Identifying key details (pages 21, 23)
1 Award 2 marks for the following details: He brought out a box of chocolate bars every day after dinner. He added to the foil ball which suggests he continued to eat chocolate regularly.
2 It tells you about different types of shoes needed for different sports. / It compares the uses for different sporting shoes.
3 Award 1 mark each for underlining any two of the following: animal or plant is usually buried under something soft; water fills the inside of the body and the soft parts rot away; the hard parts, such as the skeleton, are left behind; the sand and mud build up in layers and eventually turn to rock.
4 Award 1 mark each for any two of the following: Ariel could fly. / Only Prospero could see him. / Ariel had magic powers.

Summarising main ideas (pages 25, 27)
1 tick: Jess had been waiting a long time.
2 Plants in the forest are used as natural medicines / to cure illnesses. / Gabriela learned more about the medicinal uses of plants in the forest each time she returned.
3 Trying to survive / make a new life for himself (by building a shelter for a home and knowing what is available to eat).

Making inferences (pages 29, 31)
1 They were terrified that the dragons might start fighting again and they would be washed into the sea. / They were terrified in case they couldn't make it to the headland if the dragons started fighting again.
2 Any two of the following: It has only had one owner so it's been looked after. / It hasn't travelled far (low mileage). / It is powerful (two or four horsepower). / It is equipped for fighting (sharp knives). / It looks good (red bodywork inlaid with bones).
3 tick: To eat children.
4 tick: Fertile soil is created as a result of volcanic eruptions.

Explaining inferences (page 33, 35)
1 Award 1 mark each for any two of the following: George had possibly returned from Scout Camp, ('George was at Scout Camp wasn't he?'). / He had made himself something to eat because the kitchen was a mess and the doughnuts were his favourite. / He was really hungry or he had friends round as there was, 'far too much food here for one person alone'.
2 Award 2 marks for one reason and one piece of evidence from the text that explains why it is a good title. Reason: It is a good title because all of the things or actions in the poem explain, or are about, what the squirrel does. Evidence (quote or paraphrase from the text): It races through the woods (accept any actions from the text). Award 1 mark for an undeveloped response, e.g. It is about squirrels, or for just a reason or evidence on its own.

3 Answers related to the importance of the subjects for technologies in the future:
Children are growing up in a world where space travel is possible so these subjects will help them. / Space-related jobs might be a normal thing when the children grow up. / Space-related jobs might replace computing jobs as we know them. / They are all subjects that might help when considering working in the fields of space research.

4 Award 2 marks for a developed response referring to the text: He was upset / devastated / angry because he would never leave the horse's side which means he loved the horse like a member of the family. / His own father sold the horse which must have made him feel worse.
Award 1 mark for an undeveloped point: He felt angry / upset / lied to.

Predicting (page 37)

1 Award 1 mark for answers that say that the trees will be laden with leaves or that autumn will start again next year.

Understanding texts (pages 39, 41)

1 Award 1 mark each for any two of the following points: loads to do; fascinating animals; petting farm; brilliant rides.

2 Award 1 mark each for any two of the following points: be well prepared; complete your homework the night before; go to bed early (reasonable time); wake up early; get something to eat before the day begins.

3 tick: dehydration

4 Award 1 mark for identifying the exact words 'never gets tired'. Also accept '(unlike other muscles) never gets tired'. Do not accept the addition of any other words or the omission of any of the words outside the brackets. Any of the words in the brackets can be omitted.

Understanding fiction (pages 43, 44, 46)

1 a) Award 1 mark for *Helping your sister*
b) Award 2 marks for all four correct answers and 1 mark for three correct answers.
1 – Direct speech explaining what the character said.
2 – Reactions from the other characters. 3 – Key actions.
4 – Introduction to the section.

2 tick: dialogue

3 tick: to show key actions and events

Identifying and explaining language choices (pages 48, 50)

1 Award 1 mark for any response that explains that the wolf was any of the following: tired, tired out, worn out, exhausted, fatigued, drained or low (or similar response). For example, The wolf was very tired.

2 Any three of the following: smile; bridge; band; mountain. Award 1 mark for each correct answer, up to a maximum of 3 marks.

3 Award 1 mark for *(and) wide he goes*. Do not accept the whole line being copied.

4 Award 1 mark for any answers that indicate that night was particularly dark. For example, It suggests that it is really dark (or similar words). Also accept answers that indicate that the night covers everywhere due to the reference to 'big'. For example, The night covered a large area. Do not accept that it was big or like a black cat.

5 tick: a football

6 tick: conducting music

Explaining how language choices enhance meaning (pages 52, 53, 54)

1 a) It suggests that it is very hard and won't break (or similar suggestion).
b) They are bright, light, piercing, glowing, dazzling, beaming, glaring, etc. For example, It suggests that they are very bright and piercing like the lights on a car.

2 never ceases

3 Award 1 mark for each description, up to a maximum of 2 marks. No taller than a pencil, little fat belly, silk bodice, billowing pantaloons.

4 Award 1 mark for answers that suggest that he kept hitting his head or that it was a bumpy ride down.

5 He was surprised / shocked / found it funny.

6 tick: excited

7 not a soul was visible; buildings were like dead buildings; dead world; careless gesture; flame ran along the floor; very quickly caught the bare rafters.

Making comparisons (pages 56, 58)

1 Award 1 mark each for any two of the following:
You hold a sparkler but put a smoke bomb on the ground. / Sparklers create bright light. / Smoke bombs create bright smoke.

2 Award 1 mark for each comparison, up to a maximum of 2 marks. Comparisons can be implied: The number of humans has doubled. The number of insects has dropped by over half.

3 Award 1 mark for reference to any of the points below. Comparisons can be implied: The first poem is a rhyming poem. The second is non-rhyming.
The first poem is organised into rhyming couplets. The second doesn't rhyme.
The first poem is a rhyming poem. The second is a conversation poem.

4 Award 1 mark for each comparison, up to a maximum of 2 marks. Comparisons can be implied: Trips close to home are cheaper. Trips further away are more expensive. (Do not accept one trip is close to home, the other is further afield.)